Asia

Asia presents an overview of the geography of this continent and the countries that make up Asia. The teaching and learning in this unit are based on the five themes of geography developed by the Association of American Geographers together with the National Council for Geographic Education.

The five themes of geography are described on pages 2 and 3. The themes are also identified on all student worksheets throughout the unit.

Asia is divided into seven sections.

Each section includes:
* teacher resource pages explaining the activities in the section
* information pages for teachers and students
* reproducible resources
    maps
    note takers
    activity pages

Pages 4–6 provide suggestions on how to use this unit, including instructions for creating a geography center.

Congratulations on your purchase of some of the finest teaching materials in the world.

For information about other Evan-Moor products, call 1-800-777-4362 or FAX 1-800-777-4332

http://www.evan-moor.com

Author:	Jo Ellen Moore
Editor:	Jill Norris
Copy Editor	Cathy Harber
Desktop:	Keli Winters
Illustrator:	Cindy Davis
	Keli Winters
Cover Design:	Cheryl Puckett
Photography:	David Bridge, Digital Stock

Entire contents copyright ©1999 by EVAN-MOOR CORP.
18 Lower Ragsdale Drive, Monterey, CA 93940-5746
Permission is hereby granted to the individual purchaser to reproduce student materials in this book for noncommercial individual or classroom use only. Permission is not granted for school-wide, or system-wide, reproduction of materials.
Printed in U.S.A.

Evan-Moor
EDUCATIONAL PUBLISHERS

EMC 766

The Five Themes of Geography

Location

Position on the Earth's Surface

Location can be described in two ways. **Relative location** refers to the location of a place in relation to another place. **Absolute location** (exact location) is usually expressed in degrees of longitude and latitude.

> The islands of Japan are located between the Sea of Japan and the Pacific Ocean, on the eastern side of the Asian continent.

> Tokyo, Japan, is located at 36°N latitude, 140°E longitude.

Place

Physical and Human Characteristics

Place is expressed in the characteristics that distinguish a location. It can be described in **physical characteristics** such as water and landforms, climate, etc., or in **human characteristics** such as languages spoken, religion, government, etc.

> Nine of the world's fourteen highest mountain peaks are located in the Himalaya Mountains of Asia.

Relationships within Places

Humans and the Environment

This theme includes studies of how people depend on the environment, how people adapt to and change the environment, and the impact of technology on the environment. Cities, roads, planted fields, and terraced hillsides are all examples of man's mark on a place. A place's mark on man is reflected in the kind of homes built, the clothing worn, the work done, and the foods eaten.

> The use of irrigation in India has increased the country's average yearly yield of rice.

Movement

Human Interactions on the Earth

Movement describes and analyzes the changing patterns caused by human interactions on the Earth's surface. Everything moves. People migrate, goods are transported, and ideas are exchanged. Modern technology connects people worldwide through advanced forms of communication.

There has been a shift of population to cities in many parts of Asia.
This shift, plus increased industrialization, has resulted in major air pollution in the urban areas.

Regions

How They Form and Change

Regions are a way to describe and compare places. A region is defined by its common characteristics and/or features. It might be a geographic region, an economic region, or a cultural region.

Geographic region: Indonesia consists entirely of islands.
Economic region: The OPEC countries produce most of the oil used by Japan.
Cultural region: Arabic is the official language of several countries in southwest Asia.

Using This Geography Unit

Good Teaching with *Asia*

Use your everyday good teaching practices as you present material in this unit.

* Provide necessary background and assess student readiness:
    review necessary skills such as using latitude, longitude, and map scales
    model new activities
    preview available resources
* Define the task on the worksheet or the research project:
    explain expectations for the completed task
    discuss evaluation of the project
* Guide student research:
    provide adequate time for work
    provide appropriate resources
* Share completed projects and new learnings:
    correct misconceptions and misinformation
    discuss and analyze information

Doing Student Worksheets

Before assigning student worksheets, decide how to manage the resources that you have available. Consider the following scenarios for doing a page that requires almanac or atlas research:

* You have one classroom almanac or atlas.
    Make an overhead transparency of the page needed and work as a class to complete the activity, or reproduce the appropriate almanac page for individual students. (Be sure to check copyright notations before reproducing pages.)
* You have several almanacs or atlases.
    Students work in small groups with one resource per group, or rotate students through a center to complete the work.
* You have a class set of almanacs or atlases.
    Students work independently with their own resources.

Checking Student Work

A partial answer key is provided on pages 77 and 78.
Consider the following options for checking the pages:

* Collect the pages and check them yourself. Then have students make corrections.
* Have students work in pairs to check and correct information.
* Discuss and correct the pages as a class.

Creating a Geography Center

Students will use the center to locate information and to display their work.

Preparation

1. Post the unit map of Asia on an accessible bulletin board.
2. Add a chart for listing facts about Asia as they are learned.
3. Allow space for students to display newspaper and magazine articles on the continent, as well as samples of their completed projects.
4. Provide the following research resources:
   * world map
   * globe
   * atlas (one or more)
   * current almanac
   * computer programs and other electronic resources
   * fiction and nonfiction books (See bibliography on pages 79 and 80.)
5. Provide copies of the search cards (pages 69–71), crossword puzzle (pages 72 and 73), and word search (page 74). Place these items in the center, along with paper and pencils.

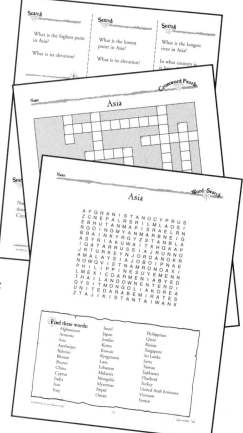

Additional Resources

At appropriate times during the unit, you will want to provide student access to these additional research resources:

* Filmstrips, videos, and laser discs
* Bookmarked sites on the World Wide Web (For suggestions, go to http://www.evan-moor.com and click on the Product Updates link on the home page.)

Making a Portfolio on Asia

Provide a folder in which students save the work completed in this unit.
Reproduce the following portfolio pages for each student:

- A Summary of Facts about Asia, page 66
  Students will use this fact sheet to summarize basic
  information they have learned about Asia. They will
  add to the sheet as they move through the unit.

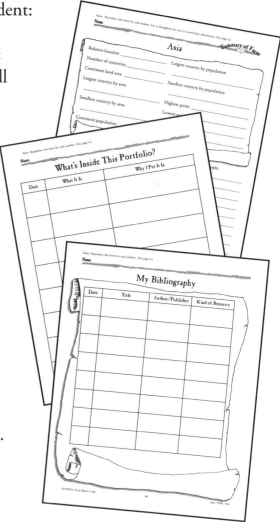

- What's Inside This Portfolio?, page 67
  Students will record pages and projects that they
  add to the portfolio, the date of each addition,
  and why it was included.

- My Bibliography, page 68
  Students will record the books and other materials
  they use throughout their study of Asia.

At the end of the unit have students create a cover
illustration showing some aspect of Asia.

Encourage students to refer to their portfolios often.
Meet with them individually to discuss their learning.
Use the completed portfolio as an assessment tool.

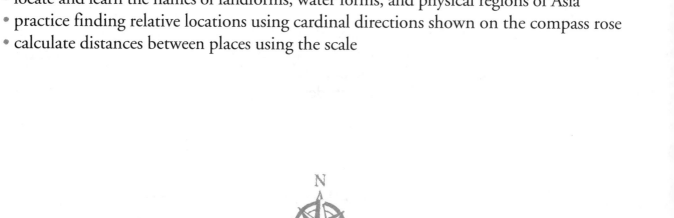

Using the Unit Map

Remove the full-color unit map from the center of this book and use it to help students
do the following:

- locate and learn the names of landforms, water forms, and physical regions of Asia
- practice finding relative locations using cardinal directions shown on the compass rose
- calculate distances between places using the scale

Introducing Asia

Tour the Geography Center

Introduce the Geography Center to your class. Show the research materials and explain their uses. Ask students to locate the sections of atlases and almanacs containing material about Asia.

Thinking about Asia

Prepare a KWL chart in advance. Reproduce page 8 for each student. Give students a set period of time (5–10 minutes) to list facts they already know about Asia and questions about the continent they would like answered.

Know	Want to Know	Learned

Transfer their responses to the KWL chart. Post the chart in a place where you can add to it throughout your study of the continent.

Where Is Asia?

Reproduce pages 9 and 10 for each student.

"Locating Asia" helps students locate Asia using relative location. Use the introductory paragraph to review the definition of relative location, and then have students complete the page.

"Name the Hemisphere" reviews the Earth's division into hemispheres. Students are asked to name the hemispheres in which Asia is located. Using a globe to demonstrate the divisions, read the introduction together. Then have students complete the page.

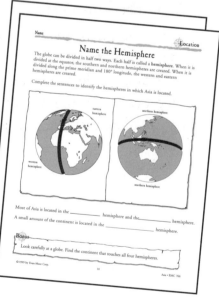

Asia

What do you already know about the unique and fascinating continent of Asia?

_____

_____

_____

_____

_____

_____

_____

If you could talk to someone from Asia, what would you ask?

_____

_____

_____

_____

_____

_____

_____

Locating Asia

Relative location tells where a place is located in relation to other places. Use the description of its relative location to help you find Asia on the world map. Color in the continent on the map below and write Asia on it.

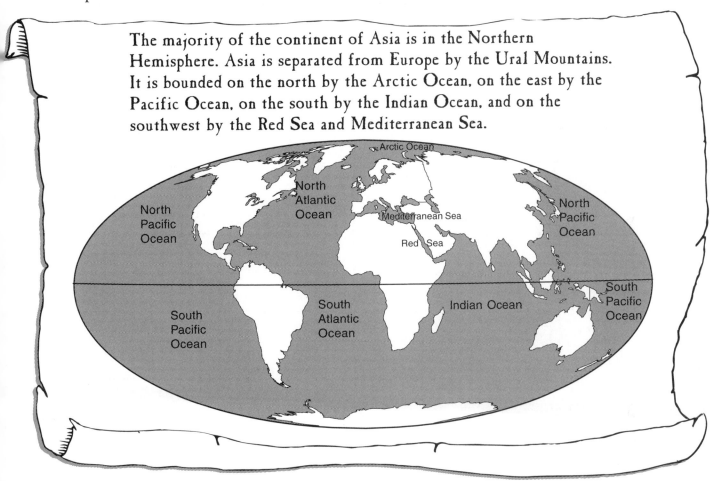

The majority of the continent of Asia is in the Northern Hemisphere. Asia is separated from Europe by the Ural Mountains. It is bounded on the north by the Arctic Ocean, on the east by the Pacific Ocean, on the south by the Indian Ocean, and on the southwest by the Red Sea and Mediterranean Sea.

Look at a map of Asia. Find these places and write their relative locations:

1. Mongolia _____

2. Qatar _____

3. Sri Lanka _____

Bonus

Write the relative location of your house.

Name

Name the Hemisphere

The globe can be divided in half two ways. Each half is called a **hemisphere**. When it is divided at the equator, the southern and northern hemispheres are created. When it is divided along the prime meridian and 180° longitude, the western and eastern hemispheres are created.

Use a globe to identify the hemispheres in which Asia is located, and then complete the sentences.

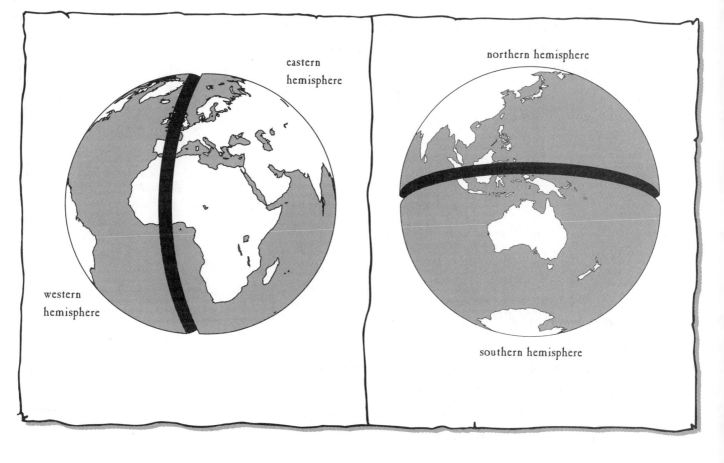

Most of Asia is located in the _____ hemisphere and the _____ hemisphere.

A small amount of the continent is located in the_____hemisphere.

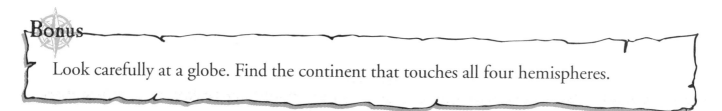

Bonus

Look carefully at a globe. Find the continent that touches all four hemispheres.

Water and Landforms

Collecting information by reading physical maps involves many skills. Pages 12–14 provide students with the opportunity to refine these skills as they learn about the water and landforms on the continent of Asia.

Water Forms

Reproduce pages 12 and 13 for each student. Use the unit map to practice locating oceans, seas, lakes, and rivers on a map.

- Review how rivers and lakes are shown on a map.
- Discuss pitfalls students may face in finding the correct names (names written along the rivers, small type, several names close together).
- Have students locate at least one example of each type of water form on the unit map.
- Then have students locate and label the listed water forms on their individual physical maps.

Landforms

Reproduce page 14 for each student. Have students use the same map used to complete page 13, or reproduce new copies of page 12 for this activity.

- Review the ways mountains, deserts, and other landforms are shown on a map (symbols, color variations, labels).
- Have students practice locating some of the mountains, deserts, and other landforms on the unit map of Asia.
- Then have students locate and label the listed landforms on their individual physical maps.

Name _____

Asia

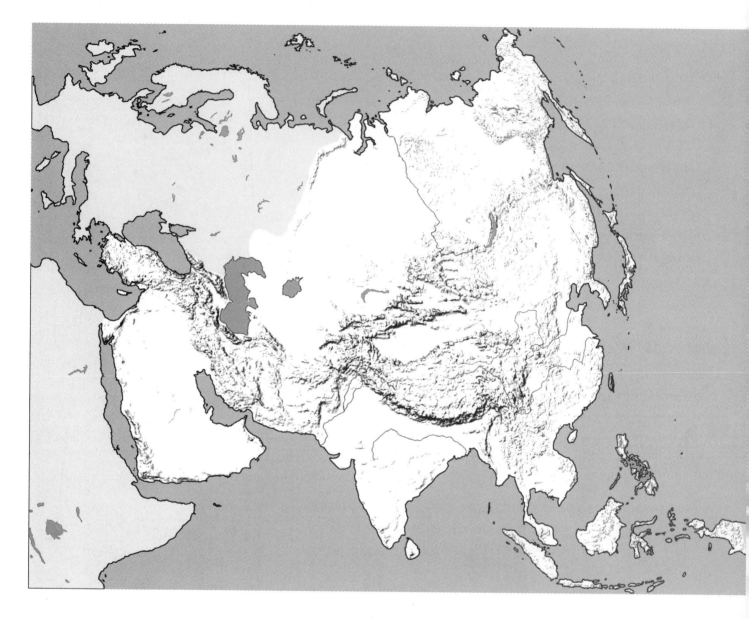

Water Forms of Asia

Find these places on your map of Asia and label them. Use a map, a globe, or an atlas to help you find the answers. Check off each one as you label it.

☐ Indian Ocean   ☐ Indus River

☐ Pacific Ocean   ☐ Lake Baikal

☐ Yellow Sea   ☐ Arabian Sea

☐ Sea of Japan   ☐ Huang He (Yellow) River

☐ Sea of Okhotsk   ☐ Bay of Bengal

☐ Ganges River   ☐ Aral Sea

☐ Yangtze River   ☐ Lake Balkhash

☐ Yenisey River   ☐ Persian Gulf

     ☐ Gulf of Oman

Trace the rivers dark blue.

Color the lakes dark blue.

Color the seas, oceans, and gulfs light blue.

Bonus

Imagine you are traveling in a small ship. Explain the route you would follow to get from Bangladesh to Taiwan.

Place

Asian Landforms

Find these places on your map of Asia and label them. Use a map, a globe, or an atlas to help you find the answers. Check off each one as you label it.

☐ Kunlun Mountains   ☐ Deccan Plateau

☐ Gobi Desert   ☐ Arabian Peninsula

☐ Plateau of Tibet   ☐ Manchurian Plain

☐ Himalaya Mountains   ☐ Ural Mountains

☐ Siberia   ☐ Zagros Mountains

☐ Tien Shan   ☐ Great Indian Desert

☐ Taklimakan Desert   ☐ Altai Mountains

Bonus

List the landforms you would cross going from Nepal to Mongolia.

Geographic Regions

Asia is a large continent with many different geographic regions. Each region has distinct physical characteristics and climatic conditions. The material on pages 16 and 17 explores some of these regions.

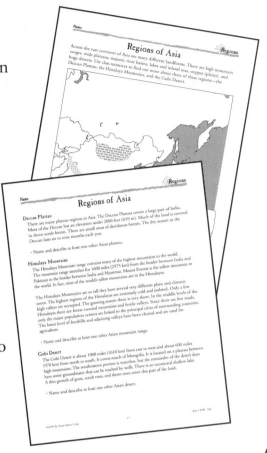

Regions of Asia

Reproduce pages 16 and 17 for each student. As a class, discuss the material about physical regions, referring to the unit map to locate each region.

Comparing Regions

Prepare a large chart on butcher paper (see below). Have students work together to fill in each box using the information gathered as they study the various regions. Do additional research using class resources to fill in any missing information. Then have each student select one of the regions on the chart, synthesize the information that has been gathered, and write a report about the region.

	Deccan Plateau	Himalaya Mts.	Gobi Desert
Location			
Climate			
Plants in the region			
Animals living in the region			
People living in the region			
Ways people have changed the region			

Name

Regions of Asia

Across the vast continent of Asia are many different landforms. There are high mountain ranges, wide plateaus, majestic river basins, lakes and inland seas, steppes (plains), and huge deserts. Use class resources to find out more about three of these regions—the Deccan Plateau, the Himalaya Mountains, and the Gobi Desert.

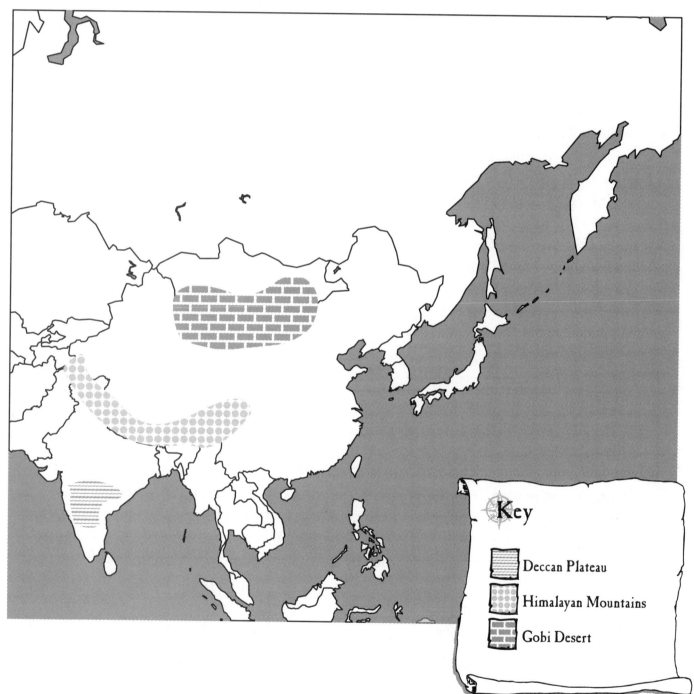

Key

Deccan Plateau

Himalayan Mountains

Gobi Desert

 Asia • EMC 766

Regions of Asia

Deccan Plateau

There are many plateau regions in Asia. The Deccan Plateau covers a large part of India. Most of the Deccan has an elevation under 2000 feet (610 m). Much of the land is covered in thorn scrub forests. There are small areas of deciduous forests. The dry season in the Deccan lasts six to nine months each year.

• Name and describe at least one other Asian plateau.

Himalaya Mountains

The Himalaya Mountain range contains many of the highest mountains in the world. The mountain range stretches for 1600 miles (2575 km) from the border between India and Pakistan to the border between India and Myanmar. Mount Everest is the tallest mountain in the world. In fact, nine of the world's tallest mountains are in the Himalayas.

The Himalaya Mountains are so tall they have several very different plant and climatic zones. The highest regions of the Himalayas are extremely cold and isolated. Only a few high valleys are occupied. The growing season there is very short. In the middle levels of the Himalayas there are forest-covered mountains and fertile valleys. Since there are few roads, only the major population centers are linked to the principal cities of surrounding countries. The lower level of foothills and adjoining valleys have been cleared and are used for agriculture.

• Name and describe at least one other Asian mountain range.

Gobi Desert

The Gobi Desert is about 1000 miles (1610 km) from east to west and about 600 miles (970 km) from north to south. It covers much of Mongolia. It is located on a plateau between high mountains. The southeastern portion is waterless, but the remainder of the desert does have some groundwater that can be reached by wells. There is an occasional shallow lake. A thin growth of grass, scrub trees, and thorn trees cover this part of the land.

• Name and describe at least one other Asian desert.

Political Divisions

A political map shows boundaries between countries or between states, provinces, and territories. In this section students will use political maps to learn the countries of Asia and their capital cities, to calculate distance and direction, and to locate places using longitude and latitude.

Countries of Asia

Reproduce pages 20 and 21 for each student. Have students use map resources to locate the names of the countries numbered on the political map of Asia. They are to write the correct number by each name on their "Countries of Asia" list.

Note: Because of the vast size of the continent of Asia, maps for additional activities are divided into five divisions.

East Asia

Capital Cities

Reproduce pages 22 and 23 for each student. Students are to list the capital cities of the countries of East Asia. Have students label the capital cities on the map and then use class resources to answer questions about the countries.

Southeast Asia

Capital Cities

Reproduce pages 24 and 25 for each student. Students are to list the capital cities of the countries of Southeast Asia. Have students label the capital cities on the map and then use class resources to answer questions about the countries.

Longitude and Latitude

Reproduce page 26 for each student. Use a map to review how to use lines of longitude and latitude to determine exact locations. Then have students complete the activity independently, using their maps of Southeast Asia (page 24).

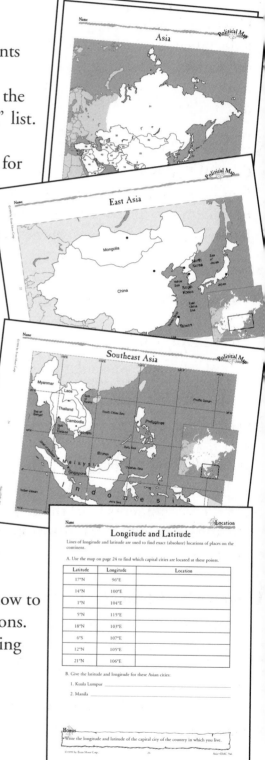

South Asia

Capital Cities

Reproduce pages 27 and 28 for each student. Students are to list the capital cities of the countries of South Asia. Have students label the capital cities on the map and then use class resources to answer questions about the countries.

How Far Is It?

Reproduce page 29 for each student. Use the unit map to review how to use a map scale to figure distances. Then have students use a ruler and the map scale to determine the distance between various places in South Asia.

Southwest Asia

Capital Cities

Reproduce pages 30 and 31 for each student. Students are to list the capital cities of the countries of Southwest Asia. Have students label the capital cities on the map and then use class resources to answer questions about the countries.

Using a Compass Rose

Reproduce page 32 for each student. Use the compass rose on the unit map to review how to determine location using cardinal directions. Then have students use their political maps to complete the activity independently.

Russia and Central Asia

Capital Cities

Reproduce pages 33 and 34 for each student. Students are to list the capital cities of the countries of Russia and Central Asia. Have students label the capital cities on the map and then use class resources to answer questions about the countries.

Country Fact Sheet

Reproduce page 35 for each student. Explain that you would like students to help create a file of fact sheets for the countries in Asia. Have each student select a different country to research. Allow time for students to share what they discover about their countries. Keep the completed sheets in a binder in the geography center.

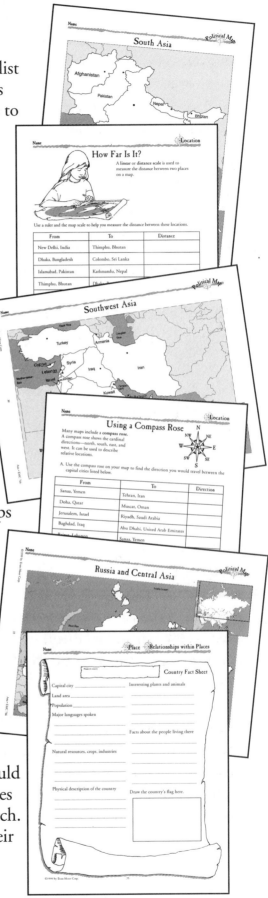

Asia

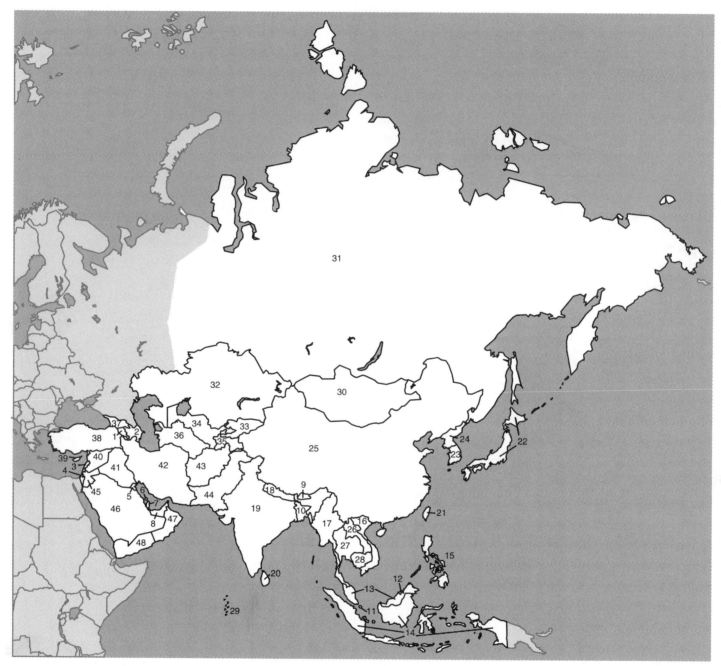

Countries of Asia

Use a map, an atlas, or a globe to help you with this activity. Find the number for each country on your map. Write the number by the correct name on this list.

___Afghanistan	___Japan	___Qatar
___Armenia	___Jordan	___Russia
___Azerbaijan	___Kazakstan	___Saudi Arabia
___Bahrain	___Kuwait	___Singapore
___Bangladesh	___Kyrgyzstan	___South Korea
___Bhutan	___Laos	___Sri Lanka
___Brunei	___Lebanon	___Syria
___Cambodia	___Malaysia	___Taiwan
___China	___Maldives	___Tajikistan
___Cyprus	___Mongolia	___Thailand
___Georgia	___Myanmar	___Turkey
___India	___Nepal	___Turkmenistan
___Indonesia	___North Korea	___United Arab Emirates
___Iran	___Oman	___Uzbekistan
___Iraq	___Pakistan	___Vietnam
___Israel	___Philippines	___Yemen

East Asia

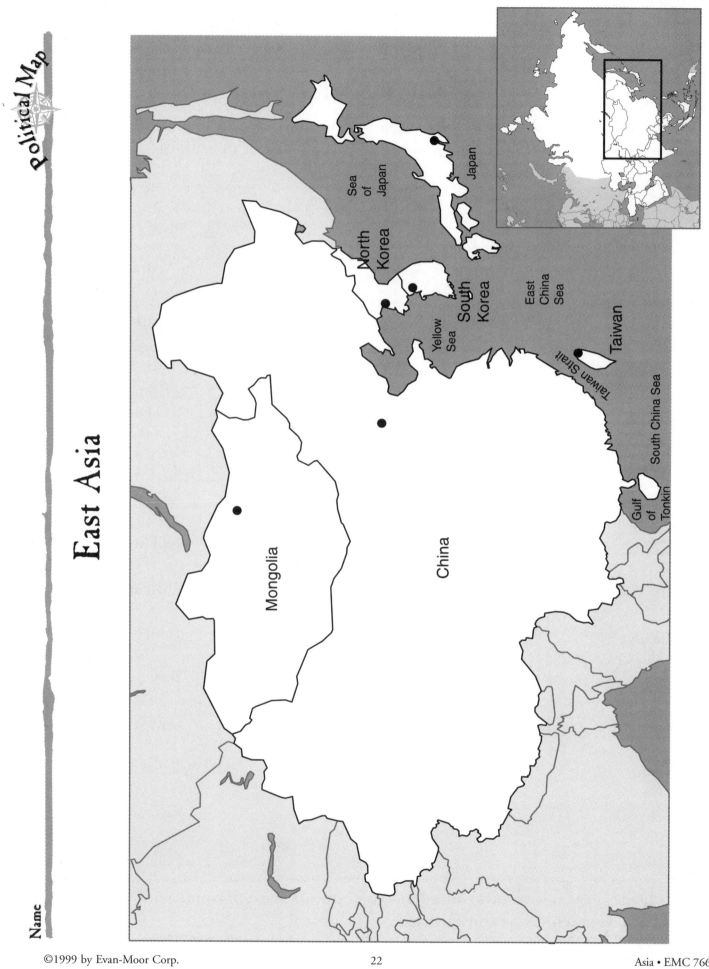

Japan

Sea
of
Japan

North
Korea

South
Korea

East
China
Sea

Taiwan

Yellow
Sea

Taiwan Strait

South China Sea

Gulf
of
Tonkin

Mongolia

China

East Asia

1. Find the capital city of each country in East Asia. Write each name here and then label it in the correct place on your map.

   a. China _____

   b. Mongolia _____

   c. North Korea _____

   d. South Korea _____

   e. Japan _____

   f. Taiwan _____

2. Name the country that is closest to East Asia. _____

3. What sea will you cross going from Japan to North Korea? _____

4. What strait will you cross going from Taiwan to China? _____

5. Name the largest island in Japan. _____

Bonus
Political divisions can be involved in disagreements between countries. Describe the dispute between China and Taiwan.

Name

Southeast Asia

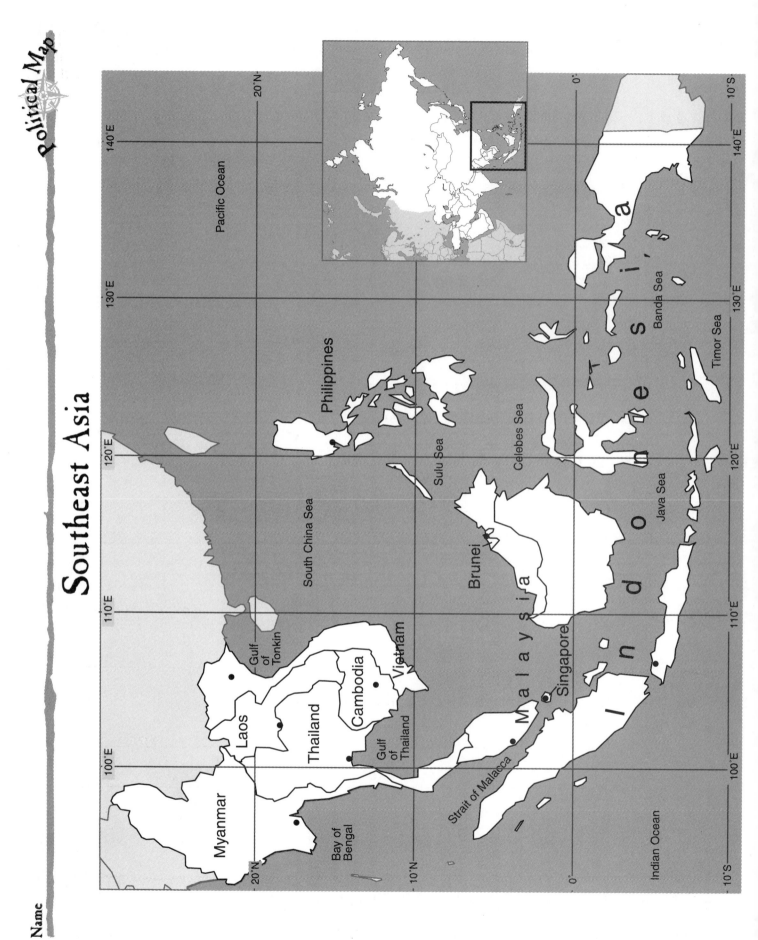

Name

Place

Southeast Asia

1. Find the capital city of each country in Southeast Asia. Write each name here and then label it in the correct place on your map.

a. Myanmar _____   f. Thailand_____

b. Cambodia_____   g. Laos _____

c. Vietnam _____   h. Malaysia _____

d. Singapore _____   i. Indonesia _____

e. Brunei _____   j. Philippines _____

2. Which countries in Southeast Asia are islands?

_____

3. What country will you cross if you travel from Yangôn, Myanmar, to Phnom Penh,

Cambodia? _____

4. What sea will you cross if you travel from the Philippines to Vietnam?

_____

5. You will often find another name given for Myanmar on maps. What is this name?

_____

6. Which countries are completely on the mainland of Southeast Asia?

_____

_____

Bonus

How do the wet and dry monsoons affect Southeast Asia?

©1999 by Evan-Moor Corp.   25   Asia • EMC 766

Longitude and Latitude

Lines of longitude and latitude are used to find exact (absolute) locations of places on the continent.

A. Use the map on page 24 to find which capital cities are located at these points.

Latitude	Longitude	Location
17°N	96°E	
14°N	100°E	
1°N	104°E	
5°N	115°E	
18°N	103°E	
6°S	107°E	
12°N	105°E	
21°N	106°E	

B. Give the latitude and longitude for these Asian cities:

1. Kuala Lumpur _____

2. Manila _____

Bonus

Write the longitude and latitude of the capital city of the country in which you live.

South Asia

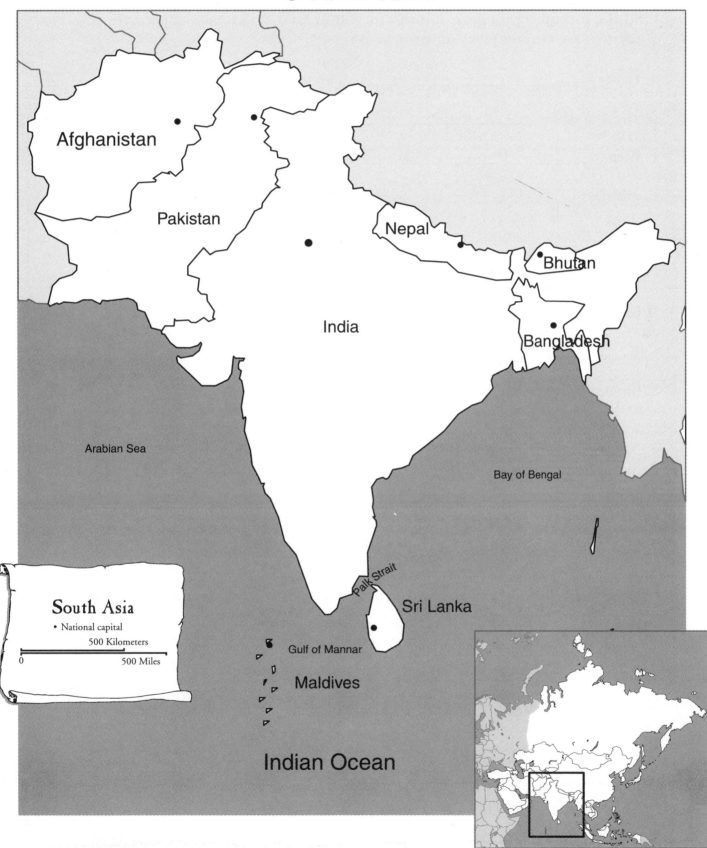

Afghanistan

Pakistan

Nepal

Bhutan

India

Bangladesh

Arabian Sea

Bay of Bengal

Palk Strait

Sri Lanka

Gulf of Mannar

Maldives

Indian Ocean

South Asia

• National capital

500 Kilometers

0   500 Miles

South Asia

1. Find the capital city of each country in South Asia. Write each name here and then label it in the correct place on your map.

   a. Bangladesh _____

   b. the Maldives _____

   c. Nepal _____

   d. Bhutan _____

   e. Pakistan _____

   f. Sri Lanka _____

   g. India _____

2. Which country in South Asia has the largest land area?

   _____

3. Which country in South Asia has the smallest land area?

   _____

4. Which country forms the border of three sides of Bangladesh?

   _____

5. What body of water would you cross if you traveled between Sri Lanka and India?

   _____

6. Which small island country is southwest of the tip of India?

   _____

7. Which island country is at the tip of India?

   _____

8. What country would you cross if you traveled from Nepal to Bangladesh?

   _____

Bonus

What countries and bodies of water would you cross to go from your hometown to India?

How Far Is It?

A **linear** or **distance scale** is used to measure the distance between two places on a map.

Use a ruler and the map scale to help you measure the distance between these locations.

From	To	Distance
New Delhi, India	Thimphu, Bhutan	
Dhaka, Bangladesh	Colombo, Sri Lanka	
Islamabad, Pakistan	Kathmandu, Nepal	
Thimphu, Bhutan	Dhaka, Bangladesh	
Kathmandu, Nepal	Islamabad, Pakistan	
Colombo, Sri Lanka	New Delhi, India	

Now find two places on the map that are about 100 miles (161 km) apart.

Bonus
Imagine you are planning to visit Colombo on the island of Sri Lanka. Use the distance scale on a world map to calculate how far it is from your hometown to Colombo.

Name

Southwest Asia

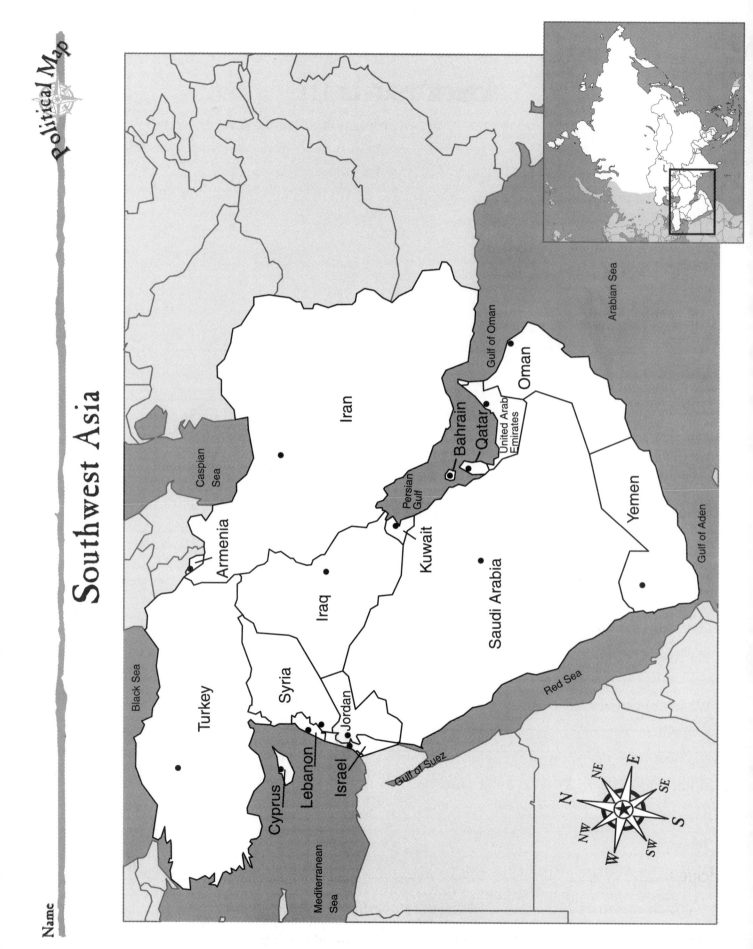

Southwest Asia

1. Find the capital city of each country in Southwest Asia. Write each name here and then label it in the correct place on your map.

a. Iraq _____

b. Syria _____

c. Israel _____

d. Saudi Arabia _____

e. Qatar _____

f. United Arab Emirates _____

g. Bahrain _____

h. Armenia _____

i. Iran _____

j. Turkey _____

k. Lebanon _____

l. Jordan _____

m. Yemen _____

n. Oman _____

o. Kuwait _____

p. Cyprus _____

2. What body of water will you cross if you travel from Iran to Qatar?

_____

3. What gulf is between Iran and Oman? _____

4. Name the island country found in the Mediterranean Sea west of Syria.

_____

5. Which countries form the borders of Iraq? _____

_____

6. What countries will you cross if you travel from Ankara, Turkey, to Kuwait, Kuwait?

_____

Bonus

Which countries in Southwest Asia are sometimes called the Middle East?

Using a Compass Rose

Many maps include a **compass rose**. A compass rose shows the cardinal directions—north, south, east, and west. It can be used to describe relative locations.

A. Use the compass rose on your map to find the direction you would travel between the capital cities listed below.

From	To	Direction
Sanaa, Yemen	Tehran, Iran	
Doha, Qatar	Muscat, Oman	
Jerusalem, Israel	Riyadh, Saudi Arabia	
Baghdad, Iraq	Abu Dhabi, United Arab Emirates	
Beirut, Lebanon	Sanaa, Yemen	
Muscat, Oman	Tehran, Iran	
Amman, Jordan	Baghdad, Iraq	
Riyadh, Saudi Arabia	Ankara, Turkey	

B. Name the sea that is west of Saudi Arabia. _____

C. Name the sea that is north of Iran. _____

Bonus

Use the cardinal directions to explain how to get from the capital city of your state, province, or territory to the capital city of your country.

Name

Russia and Central Asia

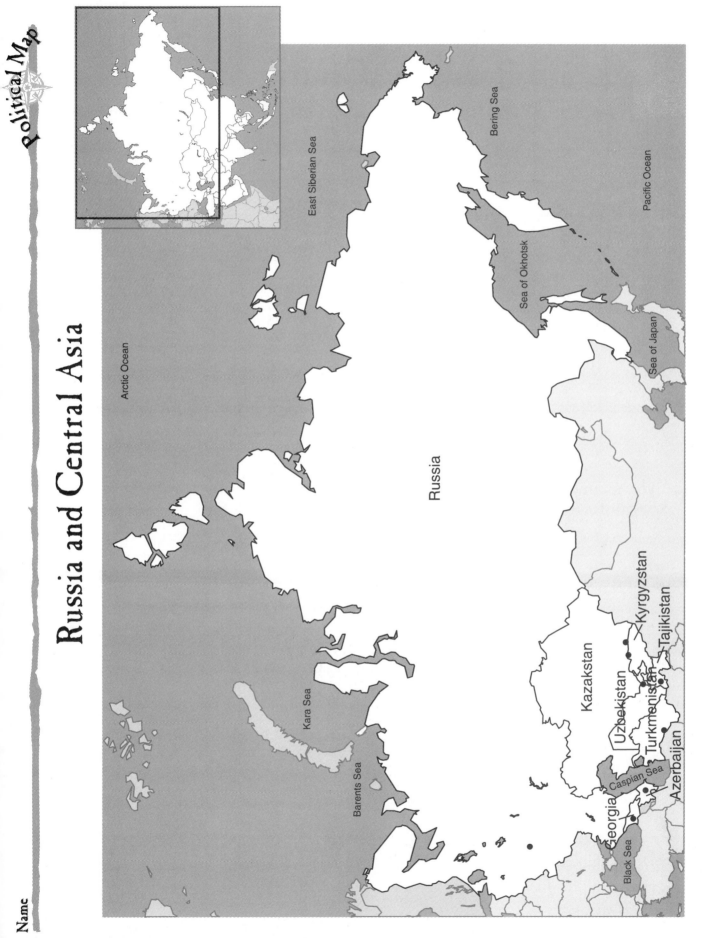

Arctic Ocean

East Siberian Sea

Bering Sea

Pacific Ocean

Sea of Okhotsk

Sea of Japan

Russia

Kara Sea

Barents Sea

Kazakstan

Kyrgyzstan

Tajikistan

Uzbekistan

Turkmenistan

Azerbaijan

Caspian Sea

Georgia

Black Sea

Russia and Central Asia

1. Find the capital city of Russia and each country in Central Asia. Write each name here and then label it in the correct place on your map.

   a. Russia _____   e. Kyrgyzstan _____

   b. Kazakstan _____   f. Tajikistan _____

   c. Turkmenistan _____   g. Uzbekistan _____

   d. Georgia _____   h. Azerbaijan _____

2. Name the oceans that are touched by Russia.

   _____

3. Which body of water is touched by Kazakstan, Turkmenistan, and Azerbaijan?

   _____

4. Afghanistan forms part of the border of Uzbekistan. What other countries in Central Asia border it?

   _____

5. If you travel from Russia to Turkmenistan, which countries will you pass through?

   _____

6. What country will you cross if you travel from Georgia to the Caspian Sea?

   _____

Bonus

The countries shown on this map were all a part of the same country until 1991. What was the name of that country?

Country Fact Sheet

Name of country

Capital city _____

Land area _____

Population _____

Major languages spoken

_____

_____

_____

Natural resources, crops, industries

_____

_____

_____

Physical description of the country

_____

_____

_____

_____

Interesting plants and animals

_____

_____

_____

_____

Facts about the people living there

_____

_____

_____

_____

Draw the country's flag here.

Asia's Resources

The activities in this section introduce students to the natural and man-made resources of Asia.

Resources

Prepare for this lesson by enlarging the political map on page 20, using an overhead projector and a sheet of butcher paper. Post the map on a bulletin board.

Reproduce page 39 for each student. Assign a country to each student or small group. Explain to students that they will be looking for information about the natural resources, crops and livestock, and manufactured goods that create the economy of the countries of Asia. (Discuss and define each of these terms before beginning the activity.) Students use atlases, almanacs, books, and the World Wide Web to locate information for the country they have been assigned, and record the information gathered on their activity pages.

Create a "key" on the map using symbols agreed upon by the students. Then have students place symbols for the items on their lists in the appropriate locations on the large map of Asia.

Agriculture

Reproduce page 40 for each student. As a class, read and discuss the material provided. Ask students that have family members involved in agriculture to share what they know about the growing and selling of crops and livestock.

Divide students into small groups. Have each group select three countries in Asia. The groups are to compile lists of the agricultural products raised in each of the three countries. Combine the resulting information into one class list of Asian agricultural products.

Extend the activity by bringing in food items that originally came from Asia. Tally the number of students that have eaten each of the items.

Burma Marketplace

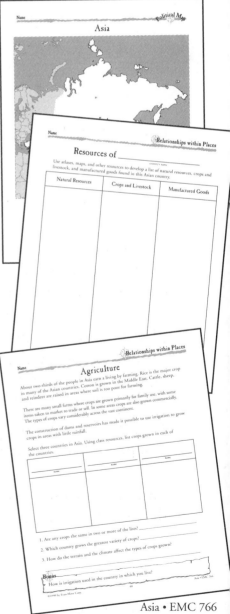

Industries

Prepare a chart on butcher paper. Divide the paper into six boxes. Label the boxes to match page 41. Reproduce copies of the page for each student.

As a class, define the terms "industry" and "manufacture." Students, working in small groups, are to use class resources to list industries of the six countries. Compile the collected information on the chart. Ask students questions such as:

"Are any industries common to all the countries?"
"Which country has the greatest variety of industries?"
"How do the natural resources of a country affect the industries that develop in that country?"
"How do transportation and communication affect the growth of industries?"

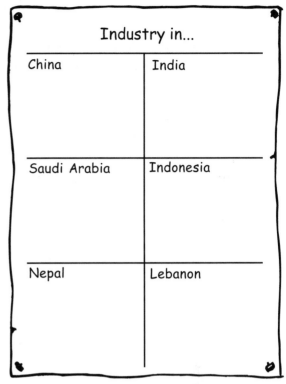

Extend the lesson by having students identify the industries of a different country in Asia.

Imports–Exports

Reproduce page 42 for each student. Discuss the terms "import" and "export" with students. As a class, write a definition of each term. Share places where information about imports and exports can be found (almanacs and/or electronic resources).

Model the activity by drawing "import" and "export" arrows on the chalkboard. Select a country. Have students find the imports and exports for that country. Write them in the correct arrows. Then assign an Asian country to each student or small group. Students use class sources to find the information needed to complete their charts. Allow time for students to share what they discover with the rest of the class.

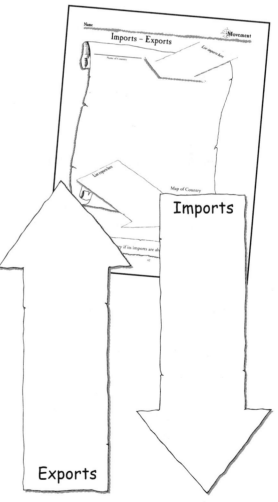

Changes

Reproduce page 43 for each student. Read and discuss the information at the top of the page together. Help students understand the concept of "developed" and "developing" countries. Discuss what is needed for these changes to occur (a fairly stable economy, roads and train tracks, access to adequate electricity and water supplies, adequate communications systems, etc.). As a class, or independently, students are to complete the page.

Vacation Time

Come to Asia

Visit a travel agency to get samples of brochures and posters about trips to various countries in Asia. After sharing these materials, have students develop one of the following:

- a brochure of things to do on a vacation to a place in Asia
- a travel poster about one special place or site in Asia
- a list of ways to be a considerate tourist
- a video advertisement encouraging people to come to some part of Asia

An Asian Vacation

Reproduce page 44 for each student. They are to plan a vacation to a place in Asia and do the following:

- select a region they would like to visit
- explain why they selected the region
- research activities available in the region
- write a letter about the trip to a friend

Resources of _____
country's name

Use atlases, maps, and other resources to develop a list of natural resources, crops and livestock, and manufactured goods found in this Asian country.

Natural Resources	Crops and Livestock	Manufactured Goods

Agriculture

About two-thirds of the people in Asia earn a living by farming. Rice is the major crop in many of the Asian countries. Cotton is grown in the Middle East. Cattle, sheep, and reindeer are raised in areas where soil is too poor for farming.

There are many small farms where crops are grown primarily for family use, with some items taken to market to trade or sell. In some areas crops are also grown commercially. The types of crops vary considerably across the vast continent.

The construction of dams and reservoirs has made it possible to use irrigation to grow crops in areas with little rainfall.

Select three countries in Asia. Using class resources, list crops grown in each of the countries.

_____	_____	_____
name	name	name

1. Are any crops the same in two or more of the lists? _____

2. Which country grows the greatest variety of crops? _____

3. How do the terrain and the climate affect the types of crops grown?

_____

Bonus

How is irrigation used in the country in which you live?

Industries

Using class resources, list the major industries in each of the following countries.

China	India
Saudi Arabia	Indonesia
Nepal	Lebanon

Bonus

How do the natural resources of a country affect the industries that develop?

Imports–Exports

List imports here

_____
Name of Country

Draw an outline of
the country

List exports here

Imports
about $_____ per year

Exports
about $_____ per year

Bonus

What happens to a country if its imports are always greater than its exports?

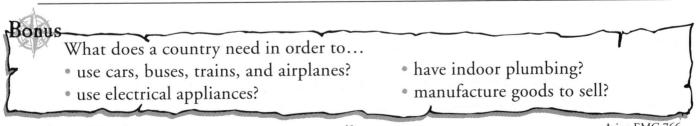

Changes

While the majority of Asian people still earn a living from agriculture, their way of life is changing. People who have lived in rural villages for generations have begun to move to towns and cities. They are entering a different work market—selling goods and becoming housekeepers, shopkeepers, miners, soldiers, or factory workers. More people are entering fields such as medicine, education, politics, and business.

Change has been slowest in isolated parts of the continent where there are inadequate transportation and communication systems. The wealth of a country, the type of government, and the existence of problems such as border disputes, war, and drought all affect the rate of development.

Use class resources to help you write definitions and then answer these questions:
1. What is a developed country? Give an example of a developed country in Asia.

_____

_____

2. What is a developing country? Give an example of a developing country in Asia.

_____

_____

3. What forms of transportation are used in less developed countries?

_____

4. What forms of transportation are used in developed countries?

_____

5. How has communication changed as Asian countries have become more developed?

_____

_____

Bonus

What does a country need in order to…
- use cars, buses, trains, and airplanes?
- use electrical appliances?
- have indoor plumbing?
- manufacture goods to sell?

 Asia • EMC 766

An Asian Vacation

Imagine you are planning a trip to Asia. Which region would you choose to visit? Why would you want to visit there? Pretend you are writing a letter to your best friend back home. Explain where you are visiting, what you are doing, and the interesting sights you are seeing.

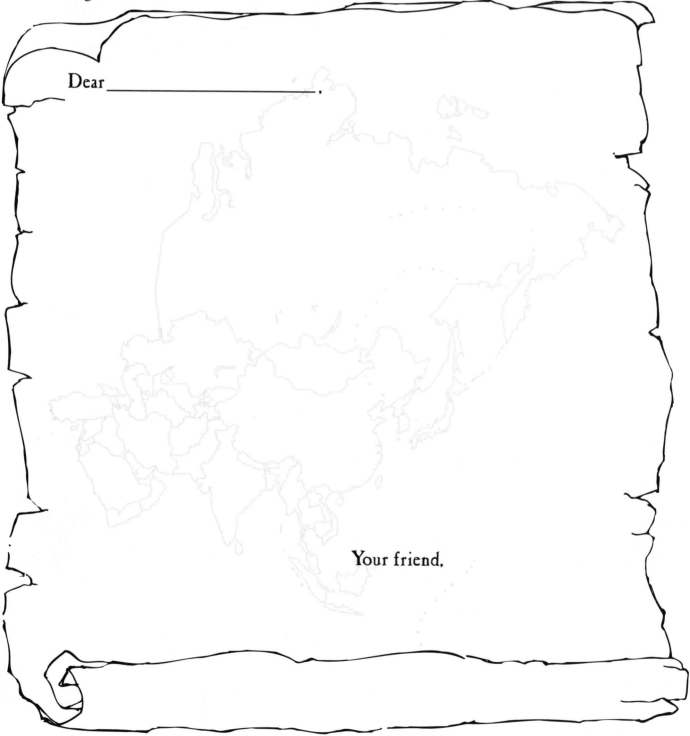

Dear _____,

Your friend,

Asian Animals

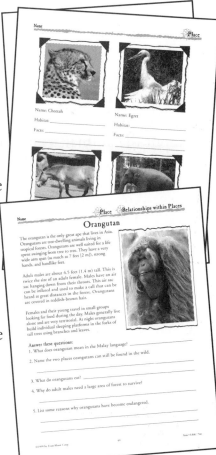

Indian Elephant

Each region of Asia has its own unique animals. In this section students will learn about many of them.

Introductory Activities

Begin by challenging students to name wild animals of Asia. List them on a chart and write a descriptive phrase after each name.

> panda—a furry, black-and-white animal that eats bamboo
> Asian elephant—a huge mammal with a long trunk and wrinkly skin
> tiger—a large wild cat with stripes
> orangutan—a big ape with reddish-brown hair

Share books or show a video about Asian animals. Discuss information learned from these sources and add new animal names and descriptive phrases to the chart.

Amazing Animals of Asia

Reproduce pages 47 and 48 for each student. Have students use class resources to locate the habitat and two interesting facts about each animal shown.

Endangered Animals

As on all the continents, there are many endangered animals in Asia. Students will learn about two of these animals, and then use class resources to find out about other Asian animals that are endangered.

Orangutan

Reproduce page 49 for each student. As a class, read and discuss the information. Have students use class resources to answer questions about the orangutan. Provide time for students to share any additional information about orangutans that they learn.

Giant Panda

Reproduce page 50 for each student. As a class, read and discuss the information. Have students use class resources to answer questions about the panda. Provide time for students to share any additional information about pandas that they learn.

Endangered Animals

Reproduce page 51 for each student. Have students use class resources to list Asian animals that are endangered. Compile a class list from the student lists.

Have each student create a poster, slogan, or song informing people about one endangered animal.

Animal Comparisons

Reproduce page 52 for each student. Have students work individually or in pairs using class resources to complete the comparison chart.

Animal Report

Provide each student with a copy of the note taker on page 53. Have students choose one interesting Asian animal and use class resources to locate information about the animal. They are to record what they learn on their note takers. Then have students synthesize what they have learned into an oral or written report.

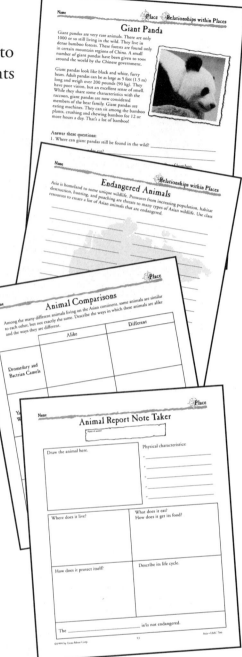

Amazing Animals of Asia

Name: Sun Bear

Habitat: _____

Facts: _____

_____

Name: Komodo Dragon

Habitat: _____

Facts: _____

_____

Name: Peacock

Habitat: _____

Facts: _____

_____

Name: Leopard

Habitat: _____

Facts: _____

_____

Name: Cheetah

Habitat: _____

Facts: _____

_____

Name: Egret

Habitat: _____

Facts: _____

_____

Name: Mongolian Wild Horse

Habitat: _____

Facts: _____

_____

Name: Asian Elephant

Habitat: _____

Facts: _____

_____

Orangutan

The orangutan is the only great ape that lives in Asia. Orangutans are tree-dwelling animals living in tropical forests. Orangutans are well suited for a life spent swinging from tree to tree. They have a very wide arm span (as much as 7 feet [2 m]), strong hands, and handlike feet.

Adult males are about 4.5 feet (1.4 m) tall. This is twice the size of an adult female. Males have an air sac hanging down from their throats. This air sac can be inflated and used to make a call that can be heard at great distances in the forest. Orangutans are covered in reddish-brown hair.

Females and their young travel in small groups looking for food during the day. Males generally live alone and are very territorial. At night orangutans build individual sleeping platforms in the forks of tall trees, using branches and leaves.

Answer these questions:

1. What does orangutan mean in the Malay language? _____

2. Name the two places orangutans can still be found in the wild.

_____

3. What do orangutans eat? _____

4. Why do adult males need a large area of forest to survive?

_____

5. List some reasons why orangutans have become endangered.

_____

_____

Giant Panda

Giant pandas are very rare animals. There are only 1000 or so still living in the wild. They live in dense bamboo forests. These forests are found only in certain mountain regions of China. A small number of giant pandas have been given to zoos around the world by the Chinese government.

Giant pandas look like black and white, furry bears. Adult pandas can be as large as 5 feet (1.5 m) long and weigh over 200 pounds (90 kg). They have poor vision, but an excellent sense of smell. While they share some characteristics with the raccoon, giant pandas are now considered members of the bear family. Giant pandas are eating machines. They can sit among the bamboo plants, crushing and chewing bamboo for 12 or more hours a day. That's a lot of bamboo!

Answer these questions:

1. Where can giant pandas still be found in the wild? _____

2. What do giant pandas eat? _____

3. Describe the giant panda's special adaptations for eating a diet of bamboo.

   _____

   _____

4. How are giant pandas and red pandas different? _____

   _____

5. Why are giant pandas endangered? _____

   _____

6. What is China doing to protect giant pandas? _____

   _____

Endangered Animals

Asia is homeland to some unique wildlife. Pressures from increasing population, habitat destruction, hunting, and poaching are threats to many types of Asian wildlife. Use class resources to create a list of Asian animals that are endangered.

_____   _____

_____   _____

_____   _____

_____   _____

_____   _____

_____   _____

_____   _____

_____   _____

_____   _____

_____   _____

Bonus

What animals in your own country are endangered?

•Place

Animal Comparisons

Among the many different animals living on the Asian continent, some animals are similar to each other, but not exactly the same. Describe the ways in which these animals are alike and the ways they are different.

	Alike	Different
Dromedary and Bactrian Camels		
Yak and Water Buffalo		
Macaque and Orangutan		
Lynx and Snow Leopard		

Name _____

 Place

Animal Report Note Taker

Name of animal
_____

Draw the animal here.

Physical characteristics:

* _____

* _____

* _____

* _____

* _____

Where does it live?

What does it eat?
How does it get its food?

How does it protect itself?

Describe its life cycle.

The _____ is/is not endangered.

©1999 by Evan-Moor Corp.

53

Asia • EMC 766

The People

Today over a billion people live in Asia. It is a continent of incredible diversity of ethnic groups and cultures, and where many social and economic changes are occurring. This section will introduce students to some of the people and some of these changes.

The People of Asia

Invite speakers from the various countries of Asia to speak to the class. Prepare students for the speakers by planning questions to ask. Appoint several students to record questions asked and answers received. Follow up the visit by writing thank-you letters.

Extend the activity by sharing all or parts of books about Asian countries as seen through the eyes of children. *Anni's India Diary* by Ann and Anni Axworthy and *Two Lands, One Heart: An American Boy's Journey to His Mother's Vietnam* by Jeremy C. Schmidt are good sources for this activity.

People of Asia

Reproduce pages 56 and 58 for each student. Make an overhead transparency of page 57. As a class, read and discuss the information page. Students are to use class resources to answer the questions on page 56. The answers may be given orally or in written form.

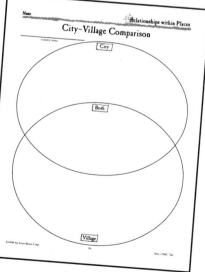

Show the transparency as a model of what students are to do to complete the people report for "How Do They Live?" Ask questions such as:
   "What country is shown on this transparency?"
   "Which ethnic groups are shown?"
   "What kind of information is included?"

Have each student select one country in Asia, use class and library resources to learn more about the peoples who live in the country, record information on the note taker (page 58), and then synthesize the information into an oral or written report. Provide time for students to share what they've learned with the class.

City-Village Comparison

Reproduce page 59 for each student. (If you plan to do this as a group activity, make an overhead transparency of the page also.) Share information about city and village life in one of the major countries of Asia using books such as *India: The People* or *China: The Peoples*. Students then complete the Venn diagram.

How Many People?

Reproduce pages 60 and 61 for each student and make an overhead transparency of page 60. Discuss the concept of "people per square mile." Students should be clear about the fact that it is an average and that some areas in a country have few people, while others are very crowded.

Show the transparency as you ask students questions about the population in various Asian countries. Challenge students to find reasons for the differences in the population sizes among the various countries. As a class, discuss questions such as:

"What are some reasons one country has so many people per square mile, while others have so few people?"

"When is it helpful to a country to have a large population?"

"When is it harmful to a country to have a large population?"

Have students use an atlas to find the populations per square mile of Singapore and Mongolia. Ask them to explain why these two numbers were not included on the graph. (The population per square mile for Singapore is so large it would take most of a page to show it; the population for Mongolia is so small it would round down to zero.)

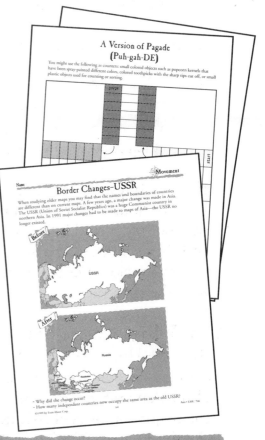

Games People Play

Reproduce page 62 for each student. Make one or more playing boards by copying page 63 and gluing it to a piece of cardboard. For each game board you will need two dice, each marked 1, 3, 4, and 6 (cover up the 2 and 5 with tape) and 16 pawns (4 each of four different colors).

As a class, read and discuss page 62. Ask students who have played hopscotch or Sorry!® to explain to the class how the games are similar to and different from Paandi and Pagade. Provide time for students to play the games.

Border Changes–USSR

Reproduce page 64 for each student. As a class, read and discuss the information, and then have students use class resources to answer the two questions. Allow time for students to share what they learn.

The People of Asia

Asia is a huge continent with a wide variety of ethnic groups. In fact, there are more ethnic groups in Asia than on any other continent. Each group has its own history, culture, and customs.

Filipino Children

Where Do They Live?

In most Asian countries, the majority of people still live in small rural settlements. But this is changing, as there has been rapid growth in cities. In a few countries, Japan for example, the majority of people live in cities.

In the northern and central parts of the continent, much of the land has a low population. The majority of people live in the southeast part of Asia. Most people in these areas live along rivers or other transportation sources such as railroads.

  • Think of a reason why so few people live in the northern and central parts of the continent.

What Languages Do They Speak?

Chinese is the most commonly spoken language in Asia. It has been taught to all the people of China to aide communication in a country with over 50 different ethnic groups speaking many different languages. Most countries have one or sometimes two official languages, but other languages are spoken by various ethnic groups living in the country.

  • Find the languages spoken by the people in these countries:

    1. Armenia _____   5. Pakistan _____

    2. Iran _____   6. Lebanon _____

    3. Cambodia _____   7. Kyrgyzstan _____

    4. Jordan _____   8. Singapore _____

How Do They Live?

The way of life varies depending on the location. Climate, available resources, and customs of a people affect their homes, clothing, activities, and relationships.

  • Use class resources to learn about the people of one of the countries of Asia. Record the information on your note taker. Share what you learn with your classmates.

Facts about the people of
China

Name of Group	Location	Facts about the Group
Han Chinese	all over China	• over 90% of Chinese are Han • Mandarin is the official language • extended families include grandparents, aunts, uncles, and cousins • strong sense of respect for elders • live in many kinds of homes from traditional to apartments to sampans on river • cities are very modern; villages are not so modern • agriculture in rural areas; industries around large towns and cities
Kazaks	northwest of China in Xinjiang and in desert provinces such as Gansu	• a nomadic people who travel from place to place to find food and land to graze their flocks • raise flocks of sheep and goats • live in dome-shaped tents called yurts which can be taken apart to move • have few possessions since they move so much • use colorful, handwoven wall hangings and rugs to decorate the tent

There are 54 more national groups of people in China.

People Note Taker

Facts about the people of

_____
name of country

Name of Group	Location	Facts about the Group

City–Village Comparison

_____
country name

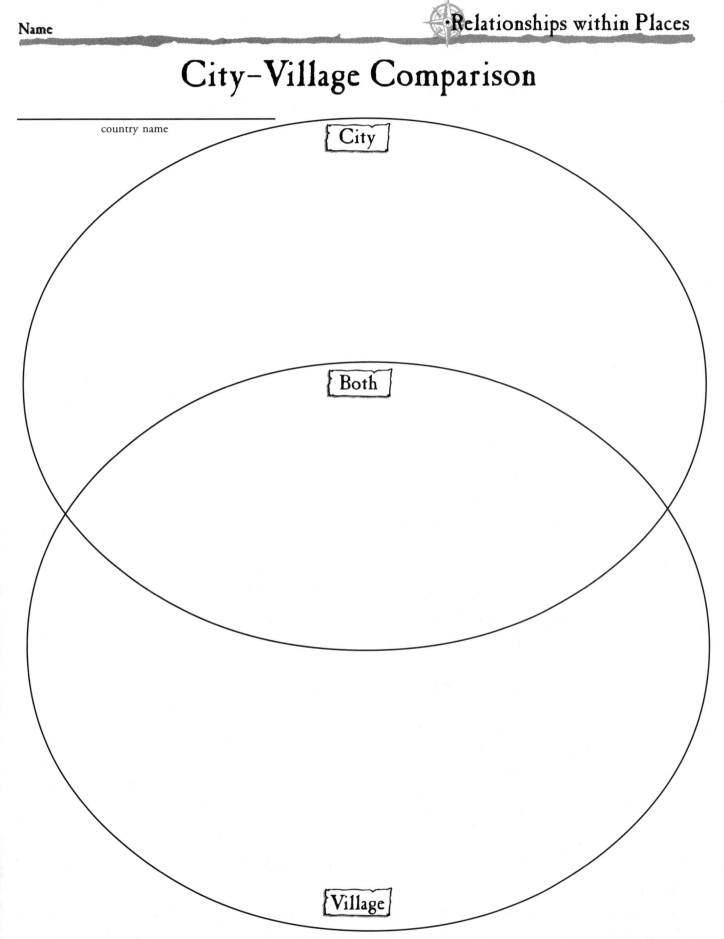

City

Both

Village

59

How Many People?—A Pictograph

(These are 1997 figures rounded to the nearest 10.)
The figures represent the number of people per square mile.

= 1000 = 100 = 50 = 10

Afghanistan	Japan	Russia
Armenia	Jordan	Saudi Arabia
Azerbaijan	Kazakstan	South Korea
Bahrain	Kuwait	Sri Lanka
Bangladesh	Kyrgyzstan	Syria
Bhutan	Laos	Taiwan
Brunei	Lebanon	Tajikistan
Cambodia	Malaysia	Thailand
China	Maldives	Turkey
Cyprus	Myanmar	Turkmenistan
Georgia	Nepal	United Arab Emirates
India	North Korea	Uzbekistan
Indonesia	Oman	Vietnam
Iran	Pakistan	Yemen
Iraq	Philippines	What is the population per square mile of... Singapore? _____ Mongolia? _____
Israel	Qatar	

How Many People?

Use the pictograph to answer these questions:

1. Which country on the pictograph has the largest population per square mile?

_____

2. Which countries on the pictograph have the smallest population per square mile?

_____

3. Which countries have a population per square mile that is less than 100?

_____

_____

4. China and Russia have large land areas. Do they also have large populations per square mile?

_____

5. Qatar and Bahrain have small land areas. Do they also have small populations per square mile?

_____

6. Is there a relationship between the size of a country and the size of its population? What conditions can affect the size of the population?

_____

_____

_____

Bonus

Find the population and the area in square miles of the state in which you live. Determine the population per square mile by dividing the population by the area in square miles. Write the population using the pictograph symbols.

Games People Play

As people travel or migrate to new countries, they carry with them many aspects of their culture. Favorite foods, music, religious beliefs, and traditions are carried along with household and personal belongings. Children carry parts of their culture too. The following games are played in Asia. Do they remind you of games you have played? Many versions of some games have moved around the world. The games may have different names and slightly different rules, but the basic games remain the same. Follow the directions to play these games from India with your classmates.

Paandi (Paahn-DEE)

Paandi is from India. It is played the same way as hopscotch. The "court" can be drawn in two different ways.

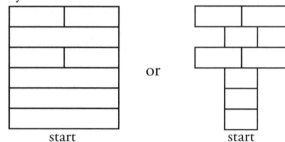

In the first round, each player throws a stone on the first space (then the second space, third space, and so on) and hops back and forth on one foot, avoiding the space with the stone. In the second round, each player throws the stone to claim a "home." The player's initials are written in the home space. Then the game is played as in the first round, except Player Two cannot step on Player One's home, and vice versa. Note that each time a player has completed a full round successfully, he or she claims an additional home space. The game is over when no one can complete a round. The player with the most home spaces is the winner.

Pagade (Puh-gah-DE)

This game is a popular board game in India among children of all ages. It is similar to the American game Sorry!®. These directions are for a simplified version of Pagade. You will need a game board, dice, and playing pieces (pawns).

1. Place your four pawns at "start." The object of the game is to get all of your players around the entire board counterclockwise and into the "home" space.
2. On your turn, roll the dice. Find the sum of the numbers shown on the dice. Move one pawn that many spaces. Or, move one pawn the number of spaces on the first die and another pawn the number on the second die. (If you roll two blanks, you cannot move for that turn at play.)
3. If you land on a space occupied by an opponent's pawn, your opponent's pawn is sent back to "start." If two of your pawns are on the same space, they are called a "pair." A pair can send a single pawn back to "start," but only a pair can send another pair back. Pairs can play together if you roll a double. Pairs can split up anytime.

A Version of Pagade
(Puh-gah-DE)

You might use the following as counters: small colored objects such as popcorn kernels that have been spray-painted different colors, pieces of colored toothpicks, or other small plastic objects.

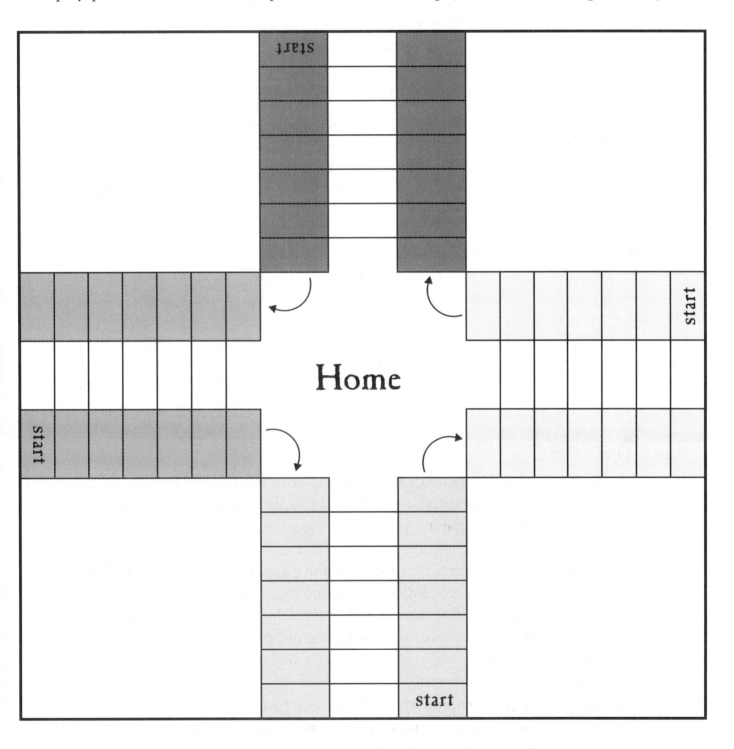

Border Changes–USSR

When studying older maps you may find that the names and boundaries of countries are different than on current maps. A few years ago, a major change was made in Asia. The USSR (Union of Soviet Socialist Republics) was a huge Communist country in northern Asia. In 1991 major changes had to be made to maps of Asia—the USSR no longer existed.

• Why did the change occur?

• How many independent countries now occupy the same area as the old USSR?

Celebrate Learning

Choose one or all of the following activities to celebrate the culmination of your unit on Asia. Use the activities to help assess student learning.

Have a Portfolio Party

Invite parents and other interested people to a "portfolio party" where students will share their completed portfolios, as well as other projects about Asia.

Write a Book

A student can make a book about Asia. It might be one of the following:
* an alphabet book of Asian people, places, or plants and animals
* a dictionary of words pertaining to Asia
* a pop-up book of the unique animals of Asia

Interview an Asian

A student can interview someone from an Asian country or someone who has visited there. The interview could be presented live, as a written report, or videotaped to share with the class.

Create a Skit

One or more students can write and present a skit about an interesting event or period in Asian history.

Paint a Mural

One or more students can paint a mural showing one region of Asia. A chart of facts about the region should accompany the mural.

Share an Artifact Collection

Students can bring in one or more artifacts representative of Asia. A written description of each artifact should be included in the display.

Sing and Dance

Present a song (perhaps the national anthem or a traditional folk song) or a dance from a region or country in Asia.

Name _____

Summary of Facts

Asia

Relative location _____

Number of countries _____

Continent land area _____

Largest country by area

_____

Smallest country by area

_____

Continent population _____

Largest country by population

_____

Smallest country by population

_____

Highest point _____

Lowest point _____

Longest river _____

Largest island _____

Interesting facts about the continent's regions:

* _____

* _____

* _____

* _____

* _____

Interesting facts about the plant and animal life:

* _____

* _____

* _____

* _____

* _____

Interesting facts about the people:

* _____

* _____

* _____

* _____

Name

What's Inside This Portfolio?

Date	What It Is	Why I Put It In

Name

My Bibliography

Date	Title	Author/Publisher	Kind of Resource

Asia • EMC 766

What is the highest point in Asia?

What is its elevation?

1

What is the lowest point in Asia?

What is its elevation?

2

What is the longest river in Asia?

In what country is it located?

3

What is the name of the mountain range that separates the European part of Russia from the Asian part of Russia?

4

This Asian country has the same name as the world's smallest ocean.

5

Name the Asian country through which the equator passes.

6

Name the Asian country through which the Arctic Circle passes.

7

Name the four major islands of Japan.

8

What is a kibbutz and where would one be found?

9

In what Chinese city
will you find the
"Forbidden City"?

10

Name the river in India
that is thought to be
sacred by Hindus.

11

Name the body of water
between...
a. the Philippines and
   Vietnam
b. India and Oman
c. India and Myanmar

12

How many countries
border China?

Name them.

13

Name this church and tell
where it is located.

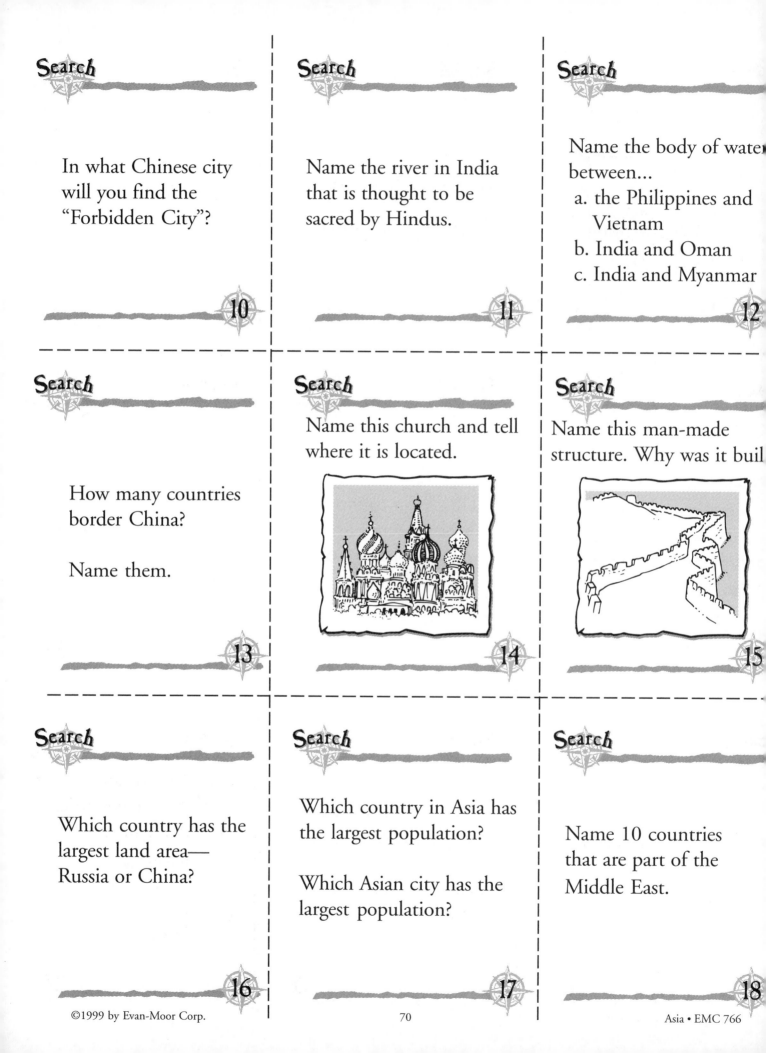

14

Name this man-made
structure. Why was it buil

15

Which country has the
largest land area—
Russia or China?

16

Which country in Asia has
the largest population?

Which Asian city has the
largest population?

17

Name 10 countries
that are part of the
Middle East.

18

Name this building and the country in which it is found.

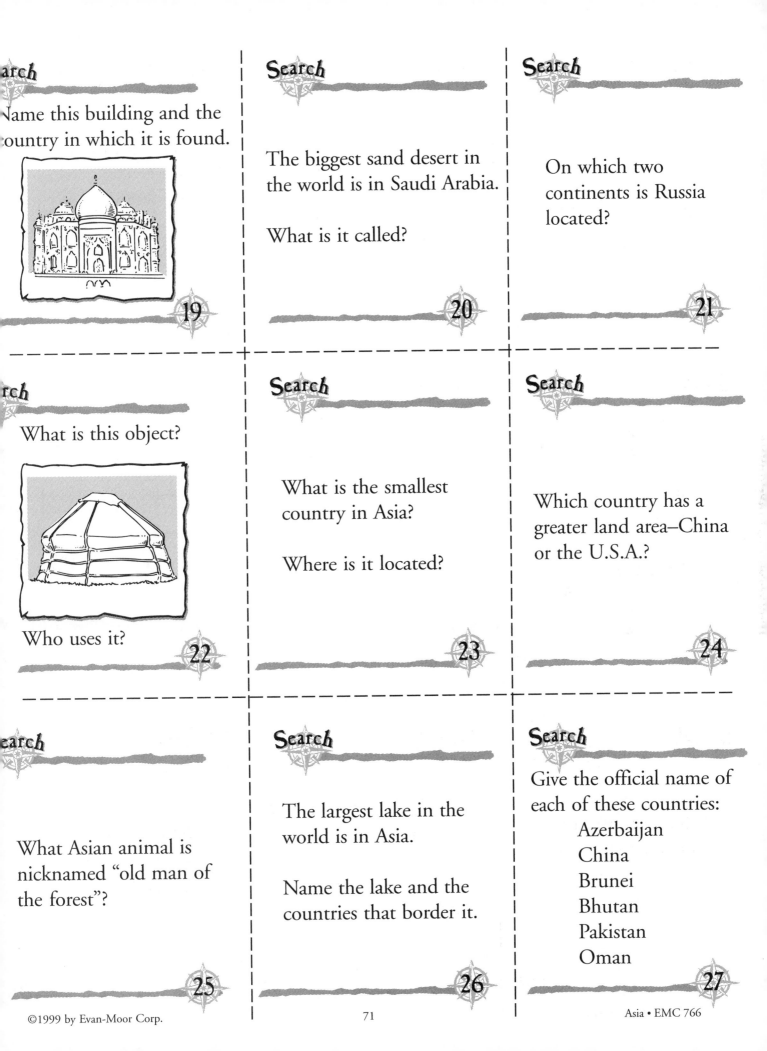

19

The biggest sand desert in the world is in Saudi Arabia.

What is it called?

20

On which two continents is Russia located?

21

What is this object?

Who uses it?

22

What is the smallest country in Asia?

Where is it located?

23

Which country has a greater land area–China or the U.S.A.?

24

What Asian animal is nicknamed "old man of the forest"?

25

The largest lake in the world is in Asia.

Name the lake and the countries that border it.

26

Give the official name of each of these countries:
   Azerbaijan
   China
   Brunei
   Bhutan
   Pakistan
   Oman

27

Asia

Word Box

archipelago

Asia

Bengal

Caspian

China

chopsticks

continents

Gobi

Hanoi

hot

Iran

map

Mount Everest

ocean

panda

Russia

Sri Lanka

Across

4. a large group or chain of islands

6. the Bay of _____ separates India and Myanmar

7. a black and white bamboo-eating mammal found only in China

11. a vast body of salt water

13. the island country found off the tip of India

14. Asia is the largest of the seven _____

15. the opposite of cold

16. the largest country in Asia

Down

1. a flat representation of the Earth

2. the second largest country in Asia

3. the highest point in Asia

5. the _____ Sea is located in northwestern Asia

8. one of the seven continents

9. eating utensils used in many Asian countries

10. a large desert in China and Mongolia

12. Tehran is the capital of this middle eastern country

15. the capital city of Vietnam

Word Search

Asia

```
A F G H A N I S T A N O C Y P R U S
Z C N E P A L R S R I L M L A O S I
E B H U T A N M A P I S R A E L R N
R G O I N G M Y A N M A R B N E I G
B R A I N K Y R G Y Z S T A N B L A
A S Y R I A K U W A I T X H Q A A P
I Q A T A R R U S S I A J R U N N O
J R T U R K E Y N J O R D A N O K R
A M A L A Y S I A J O B O I P N A E
N O W Q V I E T N A M R O N O A X I
P H I L I P P I N E S U Y E M E N N
L M E X I C O A R M E N I A B Y E D
T H A I L A N D O W N E N T E R D I
Q Y S I T M O N G O L I A K O R E A
U N I T E D A R A B E M I R A T E S
Z T A J I K I S T A N T A I W A N X
```

Find these words:

Afghanistan	Israel	Philippines
Armenia	Japan	Qatar
Asia	Jordan	Russia
Azerbaijan	Korea	Singapore
Bahrain	Kuwait	Sri Lanka
Bhutan	Kyrgyzstan	Syria
Brunei	Laos	Taiwan
China	Lebanon	Tajikistan
Cyprus	Malaysia	Thailand
India	Mongolia	Turkey
Iran	Myanmar	United Arab Emirates
Iraq	Nepal	Vietnam
	Oman	Yemen

Glossary

absolute location (exact location)–the location of a point that can be expressed exactly, for example, the intersection of a line of longitude and latitude.

altitude–the height of a thing above a given reference point; the height of a thing above sea level.

archipelago–a large group or chain of islands.

Arctic–the area at or near the North Pole.

Arctic Circle–an imaginary line circling the globe at 66.5°N latitude.

bay–part of a sea or river extending into the land.

cape–a piece of land that extends into a river, a lake, or an ocean.

capital–a city where a state or country's government is located.

cardinal directions–the four points of a compass indicating north, south, east, and west.

climate–the type of weather a region has over a long period of time.

compass rose–the drawing on a map that shows the cardinal directions.

continent–one of the main landmasses on Earth (usually counted as seven—Antarctica, Australia, Africa, North America, South America, Asia, and Europe).

culture–the shared way of life of a people including traditions, beliefs, and language.

equator–an imaginary line that circles the Earth midway between the north and south poles, dividing it into two equal parts.

ethnic group–a group of people sharing the same origin and lifestyle.

gulf–a portion of an ocean or sea partly enclosed by land.

hemisphere–half of a sphere; one of the halves into which the Earth is divided—western hemisphere, eastern hemisphere, southern hemisphere, or northern hemisphere.

indigenous–native to an area; originating in the region or country where it is found.

immigrant–a person who has come from one country to live in a new country.

isthmus–a narrow strip of land with water on both sides, connecting two larger bodies of land.

landform–the shape, form, or nature of a physical feature on Earth's surface (mountain, mesa, plateau, hill, etc.).

latitude–the position of a point on Earth's surface measured in degrees, north or south from the equator.

longitude–the distance east or west of Greenwich meridian (0° longitude) measured in degrees.

manufacture–to make a useful product from raw materials.

meridian–an imaginary circle running north/south, passing through the poles and any point on the Earth's surface.

North Pole–the northernmost point on Earth; the northern end of the Earth's axis.

plain–a flat or level area of land not significantly higher than surrounding areas and with small differences in elevation.

plateau–an area of land with a relatively level surface considerably raised above adjoining land on at least one side.

prime meridian (Greenwich meridian)–the longitude line at 0° longitude from which other lines of longitude are measured.

province–one of the main administrative divisions of a country.

population–the total number of people living in a place.

rainforest–a dense forest found in wet, tropical regions.

relative location–the location of a point on the Earth's surface in relation to other points.

reservation–land set aside for a special purpose such as an Indian reservation.

reserve–public land set aside for a special purpose such as an animal reserve.

resource–substances or materials that people value and use; a means of meeting a need for food, shelter, warmth, transportation, etc.

rural–relating to the countryside.

savanna–a tropical grassland with scattered bushes and trees.

scale–indication of the ratio between a given distance on the map to the corresponding distance on the Earth's surface.

South Pole–the southernmost point on Earth; the southern end of the Earth's axis.

steppes–an extensive plain, usually with few or no trees.

strait–a narrow passage of water connecting two large bodies of water.

symbol–something that represents a real thing.

territory–a region of a country not admitted as a state (or province) but having its own legislature and governor.

Tropic of Cancer–an imaginary line around the Earth north of the equator at the 23.5°N parallel of latitude.

Tropic of Capricorn–an imaginary line around the Earth south of the equator at the 23.5°S parallel of latitude.

tundra–vast, treeless plains of the Arctic.

urban–relating to cities.

Answer Key

page 21

43 Afghanistan
1 Armenia
2 Azerbaijan
6 Bahrain
10 Bangladesh
9 Bhutan
12 Brunei
28 Cambodia
25 China
39 Cyprus
37 Georgia
19 India
14 Indonesia
42 Iran
41 Iraq
4 Israel

22 Japan
45 Jordan
32 Kazakstan
5 Kuwait
33 Kyrgyzstan
26 Laos
3 Lebanon
13 Malaysia
29 Maldives
30 Mongolia
17 Myanmar
18 Nepal
24 North Korea
47 Oman
44 Pakistan
15 Philippines

7 Qatar
31 Russia
46 Saudi Arabia
11 Singapore
23 South Korea
20 Sri Lanka
40 Syria
21 Taiwan
35 Tajikistan
27 Thailand
38 Turkey
36 Turkmenistan
8 United Arab Emirates
34 Uzbekistan
16 Vietnam
48 Yemen

page 23
1. a. Beijing
   b. Ulan Bator
   c. P'yŏngyang
   d. Seoul
   e. Tokyo
   f. Taipei
2. Mongolia
3. Sea of Japan
4. Taiwan Strait
5. Honshu

page 25
1. a. Yangôn
   b. Phnom Penh
   c. Hanoi
   d. Singapore
   e. Bandar Seri Begawan
   f. Bangkok
   g. Vientiane
   h. Kuala Lumpur
   i. Jakarta
   j. Manila
2. Singapore, Philippines, and Indonesia
3. Thailand
4. South China Sea
5. Burma
6. Myanmar, Laos, Vietnam, Cambodia, and Thailand

page 26
A. 1. Yangôn, Myanmar
   2. Bangkok, Thailand
   3. Singapore
   4. Bandar Seri Begawan, Brunei
   5. Vientiane, Laos
   6. Jakarta, Indonesia
   7. Phnom Penh, Cambodia
   8. Hanoi, Vietnam
B. 1. Kuala Lumpur–3°N,102°E
   2. Manila–14°N,121°E

page 28
1. a. Dhaka
   b. Male
   c. Kathmandu
   d. Thimphu
   e. Islamabad
   f. Colombo
   g. New Delhi
2. India
3. Bhutan
4. India
5. Gulf of Mannar, Palk Strait
6. the Maldives
7. Sri Lanka
8. India

page 31
1. a. Baghdad
   b. Damascus
   c. Jerusalem
   d. Riyadh
   e. Doha
   f. Abu Dhabi
   g. Manama
   h. Yerevan
   i. Tehran
   j. Ankara
   k. Beirut
   l. Amman
   m. Sanaa
   n. Muscat
   o. Kuwait
   p. Nicosia
2. Persian Gulf
3. Gulf of Oman
4. Cyprus
5. Kuwait, Saudi Arabia, Jordan, Syria, Turkey, and Iran
6. Syria and Iraq

page 34
1. a. Moscow
   b. Almaty
   c. Ashgabat
   d. T'bilisi
   e. Bishkek
   f. Dushanbe
   g. Tashkent
   h. Baku
2. Arctic Ocean, Pacific Ocean
3. Caspian Sea
4. Kazakstan, Turkmenistan, Kyrgyzstan, and Tajikistan
5. Kazakstan and Uzbekistan
6. Azerbaijan

page 39
Answers will vary, but could include:
Natural Resources–coal, minerals, natural gas, hydropower potential, timber
Crops & Livestock–rice, tea, wheat and other grains, cotton, pork, fish, cattle
Manufactured Goods–iron, steel, textiles, apparel, vehicles, chemicals, leather

page 49

1. man of the forest (orang–man, hutan–forest)
2. Borneo and Sumatra–Malaysian islands
3. They are omnivorous, eating both plants and animals (fruit, leaves, nuts, shoots, insects, young birds, and small mammals).
4. Males spend most of the time alone. They are very territorial and don't tolerate each other very well.
5. Answers will vary, but could include:
   forests destroyed for agriculture
   humans are killing orangutans' prey
   orangutans are captured for the pet trade

page 50

1. in small isolated areas in some mountain areas of China
2. Bamboo shoots make up most of the giant panda's diet, and it also occasionally eats some flowering plants, fish, and small rodents.
3. large, wide, flat teeth for crushing and chewing; strong jaws for crushing large stalks; a special wrist bone that works like a thumb for holding the bamboo
4. Giant pandas are much larger, black and white, and resemble bears; red pandas are much smaller, with a reddish coat with white patches and a striped tail, resembling raccoons.
5. Answers will vary, but could include:
   destruction of habitat due to the demand for land and resources by the inhabitants, illegally killed for their dense fur, low reproductive capacity
6. Answers will vary, but could include: set aside panda reserves, harsh laws for poaching, reduction of human activities in the pandas' habitat

page 51

Answers will vary, but could include:
crested ibis
Komodo dragon
Indian gavial
wolf
tiger
snow leopard
Arabian oryx
orangutan
giant panda

page 61

1. Maldives
2. Kazakstan, Oman, Russia, and Saudi Arabia
3. Afghanistan, Kazakstan, Kyrgyzstan, Laos, Oman, Russia, Saudi Arabia, Yemen, United Arab Emirates, and Yemen
4. China has a large population per square mile. Russia doesn't.
5. Bahrain has a large population. Qatar's is much smaller.
6. Answers will vary, but could include:
   the kinds of natural resources that are available, food supply and medical care, whether there is peace or war, how the people feel about large families

page 69

1. Mt. Everest–29,028 ft (8848 km)
2. Dead Sea–1312 ft (400 m) below sea level
3. Yangtze (Chang)–3964 miles (6380 km)
4. Ural Mountains
5. India
6. Indonesia
7. Russia
8. Honshu, Shikoku, Kyushu, Hokkaido
9. a community settlement, usually agricultural, in Israel

page 70

10. Beijing
11. Ganges
12. a. South China Sea
    b. Arabian Sea
    c. Bay of Bengal
13. 13–Russia, Mongolia, Kazakstan, Kyrgyzstan, Tajikistan, Pakistan, India, Nepal, Bhutan, Myanmar, Laos, Vietnam, North Korea
14. Saint Basil's Cathedral in Russia
15. Great Wall of China–It was built to hold off invaders.
16. Russia
17. country–China; city–Tokyo, Japan
18. Answers will vary, but should include: Bahrain, Cyprus, Egypt, Iran, Iraq, Jordan, Kuwait, Lebanon, Oman/Palestine, Qatar, Saudi Arabia, Syria, Turkey, United Arab Emirates, Yemen

page 71

19. Taj Mahal in India
20. The Empty Quarter or Rub al Khali
21. Asia and Europe
22. a tent used by the nomadic Bedouins in Saudi Arabia
23. the Maldives–a group of islands off the tip of India
24. China is slightly larger than the U.S.A.
25. orangutan
26. the Caspian Sea–Russia, Kazakstan, Turkmenistan, Iran, Azerbaijan
27. Azerbaijan–Azerbaijani Republic
    China–People's Republic of China
    Brunei–State of Brunei
    Bhutan–Kingdom of Bhutan
    Pakistan–Islamic Republic of Pakistan
    Oman–Sultanate of Oman

page 72

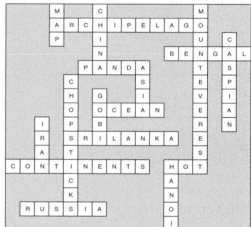

page 74

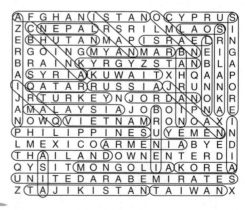

Bibliography

Books about Asia

Afghanistan (Cultures of the World Series) by Sharifah Enayat Ali; Marshall Cavendish Corp., 1995. (Also available in this series: *Cambodia*)

Asia by David Lambert; Raintree Steck-Vaughn Publishers, 1998.

The Central Asian States: Tajikistan, Uzbekistan, Kyrgyzstan, Turkmenistan (The Former Soviet States) by Paul Thomas; Millbrook Press, 1992.

Chi-Hoon: A Korean Girl by Patricia McMahon; Boyds Mills Press, 1998.

China: The Culture (The Lands, Peoples, and Culture Series) by Bobbie Kalman; Crabtree Pub., 1989. (Also available: *China: The Lands* and *China—The Peoples*) (Other Asian countries are also available: *India, Tibet, Vietnam*)

China (Major World Nations Series) by Rebecca Stefoff and Sandra Stotksy; Chelsea House Pub., 1997. (Also available in this series: *Laos*)

A Family in China (Families the World Over Series) by Nance Lui Fyson and Richard Greenhill; Lerner Publications Company, 1985. (Many other books are available in this series, for example: *An Arab Family, A Family in Egypt, A Family in Singapore*.)

Himalaya (Vanishing Cultures Series) by Jan Reynolds; Harcourt Brace Jovanovich, 1991.

India (Country Fact Files Series) by Anita Ganeri, Raintree Steck-Vaughn Publishers, 1995. (Also available in this series: *China, Japan*)

Nepal (Enchantment of the World Series) by Ann Heinrichs; Children's Press, 1996. (Many countries are available in this series, for example: *Qatar, Brunei, Indonesia*.)

Saudi Arabia: A Desert Kingdom (Discovering Our Heritage Series) by Kevin M. McCarthy; Dillon Press, 1996.

General Reference Books

(Maps and atlases published before 1997 may not have the latest changes in country names and borders, but they will still contain much valuable material.)

Atlas of Continents; Rand McNally & Company, 1996.

National Geographic Concise Atlas of the World; National Geographic Society, 1997.

National Geographic Picture Atlas of Our World; National Geographic Society, 1994.

The New Puffin Children's World Atlas by Jacqueline Tivers and Michael Day; Puffin Books, 1995.

The Reader's Digest Children's Atlas of the World; Consulting Editor: Colin Sale; Joshua Morris Publishing, Inc., 1998.

The World Almanac and Book of Facts 1998; Editorial Director: Robert Famighetti; K-III Reference Corporation, 1997.

Technology

CD-ROM and Disks

Encarta® Encyclopedia; ©Microsoft Corporation (CD-ROM).

MacGlobe & PC Globe; Broderbund (disk).

Where in the World Is Carmen Sandiego?; Broderbund (CD-ROM and disk).

World Fact Book; Bureau of Electronic Publishing Inc. (CD-ROM).

Zip Zap Map; National Geographic (laser disc and disk).

Websites

For sites on the World Wide Web that supplement the material in this resource book, go to http://www.evan-moor.com and look for the Product Updates link on the main page.

Check this site for information on specific countries:

CIA Fact Book–www.odci.gov/cia/publications/factbook/country-frame.html